T0362842

Little Red Riding Hood and the Five Senses

Retold and dramatised as a scripted play
for five to seven readers.

Ellie Hallett

Cast and suggested wardrobe

Storytellers (ST1 and ST2)	Two individuals or two small groups. TV reporter-type clothes.
Red Riding Hood (RRH)	Red cape with hood.
Mother (M)	Mother-type clothes and an apron.
Granny (G)	Night attire and a pair of glasses.
Wolf (W)	Two felt ears and dark clothing. Optional trimmings can be tail, teeth etc.
Hunter (H)	Outdoor clothing.

Note

The parts of **Mother**, **Granny** and the **Hunter** can be read by the same person, changing the voice to suit each character.

ST1	Hello! I am Story Teller One ...
ST2	... and I am Story Teller Two.
ST1	This is the famous fairytale called Little Red Riding Hood.
ST2	While we are telling this story, our five senses or the way we use them will be mentioned quite often.
ST1 & 2	As you probably already know, our five senses are ... *(ad lib extra touches here)*

SIGHT   TOUCH   HEARING TASTE and SMELL

ST1	Our senses give us important information about our surroundings. They also help us learn things and stay safe.
ST2	Without our senses, we couldn't **see**, **feel**, **hear**, **taste** or **smell**.
ST1	How awful!
ST2	And we wouldn't **feel** hot or cold.
ST1	We couldn't **see** where we were going…
ST2	… or **taste** our dinner …
ST1	… or **smell** a perfumed rose …
ST2	… or **hear** a bird sing.
ST1	Our senses are certainly **very** important!

ST2	Let's now introduce the characters in this famous story.
M	I'm Mother. I've just made a cake for Granny using the **tastiest** fruit from the apple trees in the garden.
G	*(cough)* I'm Granny. I don't **feel** at all well. I'll be in my cottage at the other side of the forest **reading** my book.
W	I am the Wolf. I'm going to stay out of **sight** behind some bushes in the forest to **watch** what is going on.
H	I am a Hunter with very keen **eyesight** and excellent **hearing**. I'm off to check for rabbits in the fields quite a long way away, so I must leave immediately.

ST1	And now let's begin our story.
RRH	That apple cake **smells** delicious, Mother dear! I can **see** steam rising so I know not to **touch** it as it is still very hot.
M	After it has **cooled**, I'll pack a basket of goodies for Granny. I'll meet you at Granny's house a bit later as I need to make another cake for your school fete.
RRH	I love visiting Granny. She'll be so happy to **see** me.
M	We have been to Granny's cottage many times before, so you know the way. All you have to do is follow the path.

M	Now remember to go straight to Granny's cottage, Little Red Riding Hood. Don't talk to strangers.
RRH	I'll remember. I'll go straight there.
ST2	And so off she went.

ST1	Little Red Riding Hood loved the forest. She **looked** for flowers …

ST2	… she breathed in the cool fresh **smell** of the trees …
ST1	… and she **felt** the breeze on her face.
SY2	She **listened** to the birds singing …

ST1	… and then **tasted** some blackberries to check if they were ripe.
ST2	She was just about to pick an unusual blue daisy for Granny when she **heard** a rustle in the bushes behind her.
RRH	That's a funny **sound!** It's probably just a little lizard looking for ants.
W	Well hello, little girl!
ST1	And a wolf slid out from the shadows.
RRH	Oh me, oh my! Who are you? My mother said I was not to talk to strangers.
W	Are you walking through the forest by yourself, you pretty little thing?

RRH	Yes I am, and I'm on my way to **see** my Granny who lives on the other side of the forest.
ST2	The wolf's voice **sounded** so smooth that she forgot her mother's warning.
W	And what is your name, sweet child?

RRH	My name is Little Red Riding Hood, and I'm off to visit Granny because she has been **feeling** unwell.
ST1	Too much information, Little Red Riding Hood! Keep walking! Do not **listen** to what the wolf is saying!
ST2	But the wolf kept on talking, and Little Red Riding Hood kept on **listening**.
ST1	The wolf meanwhile was thinking of a crafty plan, and his eyes narrowed.
W	Oh, and what a **tasty** and **sweet-smelling** little girl you are. Oops - I mean what a kind and sweet-natured little girl you are, Little Red Riding Hood.

ST2	Oh dear. Things are not **looking** good. Please, Little Red Riding Hood, do not trust this slippery character!
W	Allow me to accompany you through the forest. You never know what sort of dangers could be lurking behind the trees and among the bushes.
RRH	You're very kind Mr Wolf! Thank you.
ST1	Little Red Riding Hood suddenly **noticed** some wildflowers in a sunny glen.
RRH	These wildflowers **look** like a magic carpet. And what a lovely humming **sound** of insects I can **hear**.

W	Oh my goodness! I've just remembered a job I have to do. Goodbye, sweet thing. I must be on my way.
ST2	And so off went the wolf, disappearing from **sight** as he loped into the distance. But we all know where the wolf was going!
ST1	Let's now go to Granny's cottage to **see** and **hear** what happens next.
G	Cough cough. I hope a day in bed with my favourite book will make me **feel** a lot better. *(loud knocking)* That's a very loud knocking s**ound**. Who is it?
W	It's me, Little Red Riding Hood, your sweet-**smelling** granddaughter!

G	The door is unlocked. Come in, my dear, so I can **see** you more clearly! Oh no! You don't **look** at all like my dear little granddaughter. Help! Ahhhh!

ST2	And in one gulp the wolf swallowed Granny whole.

ST1	The wolf then climbed into Granny's **soft warm** bed.
W	Yummo! That was a very **tasty** first course! I'll now put on Granny's nightcap and glasses so that I **look** just like her.

ST2	The wolf was settling himself in Granny's bed when Little Red Riding Hood arrived.
RRH	Yoohoo! Hello, Granny! It's me, Little Red Riding Hood. I have brought you some **tasty** goodies to help you **feel** better.

W	*(softly)* And here is my sweet-**tasting** dessert. What a good plan this is!
W	Come closer my dear so I can **see** you more clearly!
RRH	Why Granny! What a long nose you have!
W	All the better to **smell** you, my dear!
RRH	And Granny, what big **eyes** you have!
W	All the better to **see** you, my dear!
RRH	And Granny, what a big **tongue** you have!
W	All the better to **taste** you, my dear!
RRH	And Granny – what big teeth you have!
W	All the better to eat you, my dear!

ST2	And in the blink of an eye, the wolf ate Little Red Riding Hood in one swallow.
ST1	Fortunately, the story has not finished yet. The Hunter's sense of **hearing** is about to save the day. Let's **listen** carefully to find out what happens next.

W	Ahh! I **feel** much better now. After all that food I deserve a little nap, especially as this bed **feels** so **soft** and **warm** and **cosy**. Mmmm ... *(starts snoring)*
ST2	The wolf's snoring was so **loud** that the hunter passing by **heard** it.
H	What a truly dreadful **noise**! It **sounds louder** than anything I have ever **heard** coming from this cottage. It can't possibly be dear Granny who is **snoring**!
SS1	When the hunter **looked** through the window, he couldn't believe his **eyes**.
H	Oh no! It's a wolf in Granny's bed. I can also **see** that he is very fat. I think I know what has happened.

ST2	The hunter rushed into the cottage and tickled the wolf so much that …
ST1	… out jumped both Granny and Red Riding Hood.
H	Well I never! Poor Granny and a little girl! You were both swallowed by the wolf.
G	Oh thank you, Mr Hunter! May I introduce my dear little granddaughter. She is called Little Red Riding Hood.
RRH	Nice to meet you, Mr Hunter. Thank you for saving Granny and me. Ohhh! It was so **dark** in there that Granny and I couldn't **see** a thing, but we did **hear** very **loud snoring**!

G	And it **felt** *really* uncomfortable with the two of us squashed inside the wolf!
RRH	Just as well you **heard** the wolf snoring!
H	But why was the wolf in your bed, Granny?
G	You won't believe your **ears** when you **hear** this! Red Riding Hood came to visit me to **see** if I was **feeling** better. The wolf was in my bed trying to **look** like me!
H	The cheek of him! Well, he certainly got a big fright when I tickled him. And I have a very good idea regarding the wolf.

G	How about a cup of tea and some **tasty** cake while we **listen** to your idea?
H	Yes please, but first I must make a delivery to a friend of mine who lives nearby.
RRH	Can we **hear** about your good idea before you go, please Mr Hunter?
H	Certainly! I know a zoo-keeper, and I **heard** him say that the zoo needs a wolf for children to **see** when they visit.
ST2	Off went the hunter with the wolf over his shoulder to deliver him to the zoo-keeper.

| G | Well, after all these adventures, I am **feeling** a lot better! |
| RRH | I will set the table for afternoon tea while we wait for Mother and Mr Hunter. |

ST2	Granny **found** a jar of last summer's strawberry jam, and she whipped some fresh cream to go with the apple cake.
G	Here they are! I can **see** your Mother and Mr Hunter coming to join us.
ST1	While they were having afternoon tea, Red Riding Hood announced in a **loud** voice …
RRH	I have decided that when I am walking by myself, I won't talk to strangers!
ST1 & 2	And – *(pause)* she never did.